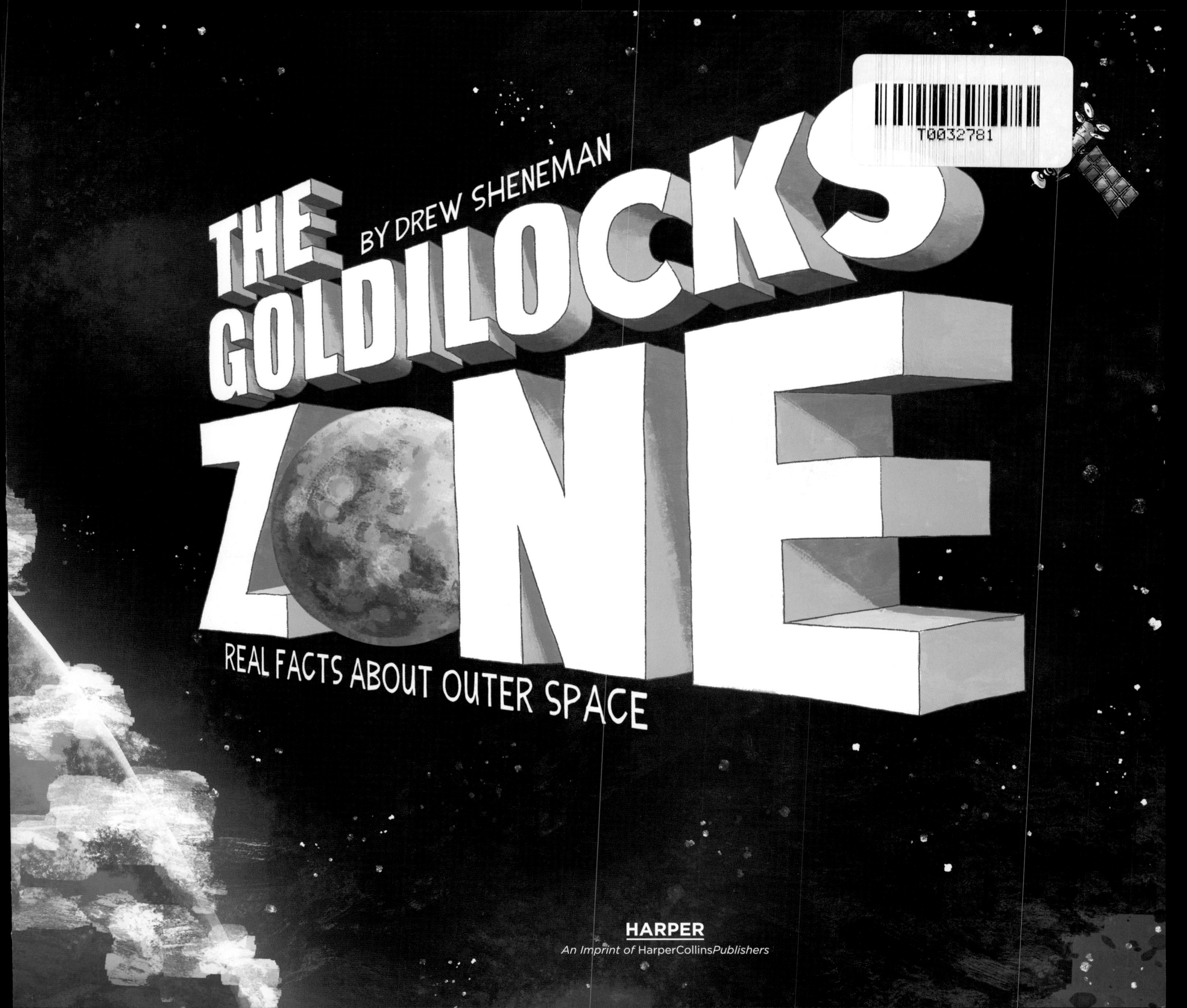
T0032781
BY DREW SHENEMAN
THE GOLDILOCKS ZONE
REAL FACTS ABOUT OUTER SPACE
HARPER
An Imprint of HarperCollinsPublishers

MERCURY
VENUS
EARTH
MARS

This is our solar system, a small neighborhood-sized chunk of the universe with our Sun at the center. There are seven other planets in our solar system, but only one Earth.

Our place in the solar system is what makes Earth such a great home. It's not too close to the Sun and not too far away.

Scientists call this
THE GOLDILOCKS ZONE.

DID SOMEBODY SAY GOLDILOCKS?
THAT'S ME!

It's called the Goldilocks Zone because Earth is the only planet in the solar system that isn't too hot or too cold for life to thrive.

That's right. If you don't believe me, ask a scientist.

IT'S TRUE! NO OTHER PLANET IN THE SOLAR SYSTEM HAS THE UNIQUE SET OF CONDITIONS TO SUPPORT LIFE THE WAY EARTH DOES.
A SCIENTIST
AH!

SEE, I MADE A CHART!
EVER HEARD OF KNOCKING?
YOU BROKE IN HERE.
1. WATER
2. NOT TOO HOT
3. NOT TOO COLD

STILL NOT BUYING IT?
I SUPPOSE I COULD SHOW YOU.
LET'S TAKE A TOUR OF OUR SOLAR SYSTEM!

First stop . . . Mercury!

Mercury is the smallest planet in the solar system. It's also the closest to the Sun. At an average of just 48 million miles from Earth, Mercury is practically just around the corner.

The funny thing is that while the parts of Mercury facing the Sun are extremely hot (about 800 degrees Fahrenheit) . . .

the parts facing away from the sun are incredibly cold (about -300 degrees Fahrenheit).

Being so close to the Sun should make Mercury the hottest planet, but that honor falls to our next stop. . . .
Witness Venus!
The brightest planet in the night sky.

So what makes Venus so hot?
OUR MIXTAPE?

Venus is so hot because its thick atmosphere traps the heat from the Sun. Scientists have sent probes to Venus, but they only lasted, at most, a few hours before their electronics failed.

If that wasn't bad enough, the air on Venus is poisonous, the lightning is frequent, and the pressure on the surface would crush you.

After Venus, the next stop from the Sun is Earth and then Mars.

VENUS:
67 MILLION MILES
FROM THE SUN
EARTH:
93 MILLION MILES
FROM THE SUN
MARS:
142 MILLION MILES
FROM THE SUN

Over the years, we have sent a number of robotic rovers to explore the surface of Mars.

While scientists haven't discovered any life on the planet, they did discover water underneath the Martian surface. Despite no sign of life today, there may have been some form of life on Mars millions or billions of years ago.

Of all the planets other than Earth, Mars would be the most livable for humans. But if we ever attempt to live on Mars, we will have to bring food, shelter, water, and even air with us.

The next group of planets are not like Mercury, Venus, Earth, and Mars. They are not made primarily of rock but instead are made of giant swirling balls of gas, dust, and ice.
THEY'RE CALLED GAS GIANTS.
THAT'S WHAT WE CALL MY DAD ON CHILI NIGHT.
JUPITER
SATURN
URANUS
NEPTUNE

If you ever traveled to Jupiter, you couldn't even stand on the surface because it does not have a surface to stand on. The planet is just a big, slushy ball of gas and ice, which grows thicker down to its core.

Jupiter is more massive than all the other planets in the solar system combined. Jupiter is so massive and its gravity so strong that it affects the fate of the other planets.

Billions of years ago, when the solar system was still forming, Jupiter started drifting closer to the Sun. When it did, Jupiter's powerful gravity may have dislodged a rock from the asteroid belt between it and Mars. Some scientists think that may have been the asteroid that hit Earth and killed the nonavian dinosaurs.

Nearly 403 million miles further out in space is the ringed planet of Saturn. If you tried to drive there from Jupiter, it would take 279,861 days, assuming you observed Earth speed limits.

Saturn's stunning rings are made of trillions of chunks of ice.

If you tried to stand on the surface of Saturn, you'd sink into a toxic soup of gas and ice until the pressure popped you like a grape.

THAT'S A HARD PASS.
Saturn is the least dense planet. In fact, it is lighter than water. If you put Saturn in the bathtub, it would float.
WE'RE GONNA NEED A BIGGER TUB.

Our next stop is Uranus. This planet might have a funny name, but you do not want to live here.

Uranus and Neptune are a lot like Jupiter and Saturn, but colder.

Both are also made of gas, but much of that gas is frozen, so scientists also call them ice giants.

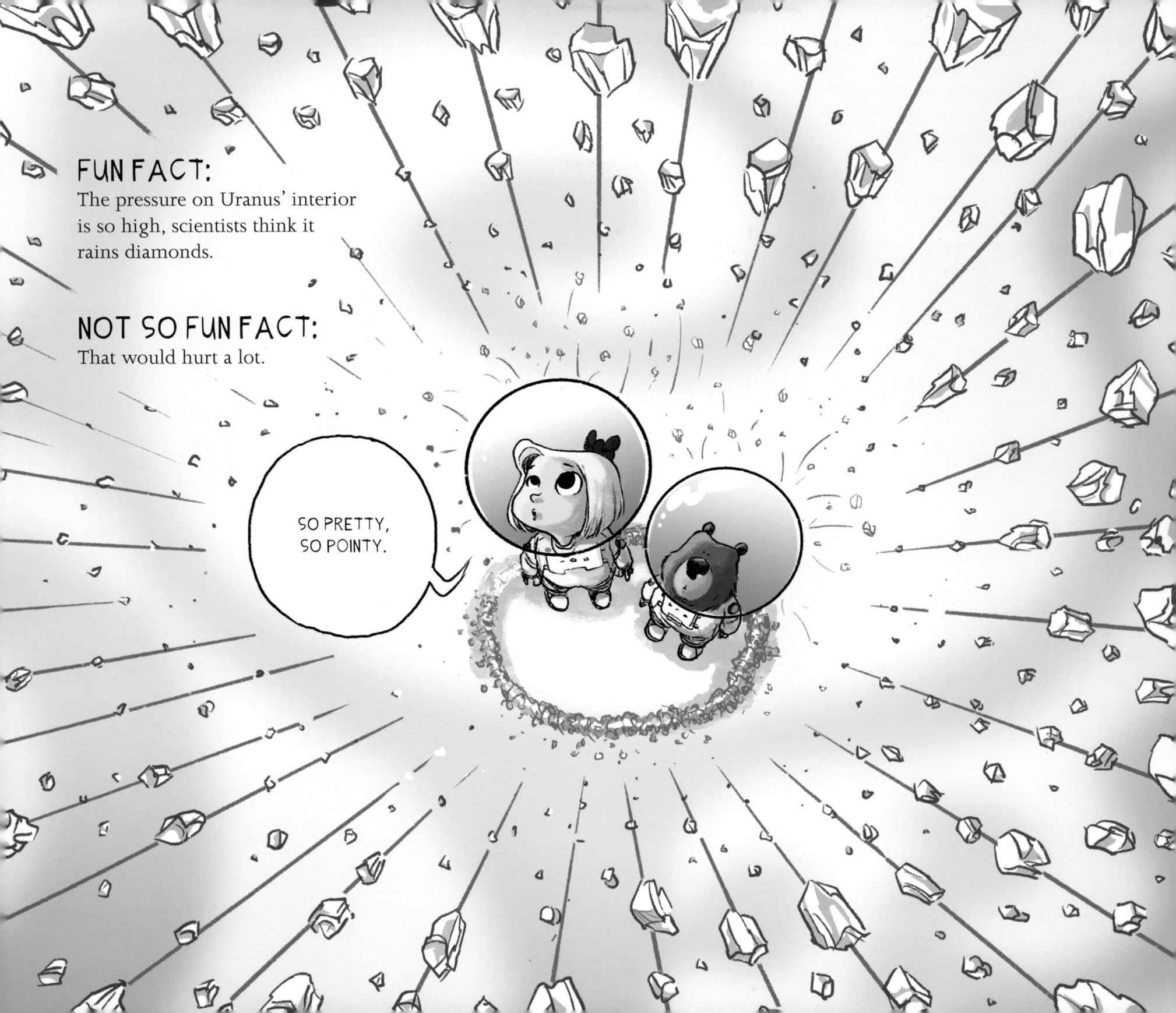

FUN FACT:

The pressure on Uranus' interior is so high, scientists think it rains diamonds.

NOT SO FUN FACT:

That would hurt a lot.

The temperature on Neptune is a brisk 392 degrees Fahrenheit below zero.

Neptune also has the strongest storms in the solar system with winds traveling 1200 miles per hour. That is faster than a fighter jet.

I PICKED
THE WRONG PLANET
TO FLY A KITE!

Neptune's atmosphere is made of hydrogen, helium, and methane. The methane is what gives it that vibrant blue color.

Far beyond the planets and the Kuiper Belt, a ring of comets, asteroids, and icy bodies, lies Pluto. Pluto was once considered a planet.

To qualify for planetary status, an object must do three things:

1. ORBIT A STAR LIKE THE SUN
2. HAVE ENOUGH MASS TO MAINTAIN A ROUND SHAPE
3. CLEAR ITS ORBIT OF OTHER OBJECTS

Pluto does the first two, but not the third, therefore Pluto is not a planet.

You know what else aren't planets? The Sun and Moon.

The Sun is a star. It provides Earth with the heat and light we need to live. Any closer would be too hot, any farther away too cold.

As for the Moon . . .

Planets orbit the Sun.
Moons orbit planets.
The Moon is not a planet.
The Moon is a moon.

At long last, we arrive back on Earth! Third planet from the Sun and the place where you keep all your stuff.
I CAN SEE YOUR HOUSE FROM HERE.

Earth has it all!
Food! Air! Water!
And temperatures that won't
cause you to burst into flames.

There is life in every nook
and cranny of Earth.

From the depths of the ocean . . .
to the tops of the highest mountains . . .

Life on Earth is diverse,
and it is everywhere!

EARTH IS THE ONLY PLANET
IN OUR SOLAR SYSTEM
WHERE WE KNOW LIFE EXISTS!

WHOA, DOES THAT MEAN WE'RE ALL ALONE IN THE UNIVERSE?

Not necessarily. The universe is an awful big place, and we have only explored a tiny piece of it. It's possible that somewhere out there, another planet is just the right place for life to thrive.

But we only have one Earth for now, so let's do our best to take care of it.

PLANET

JUPITER:
NAMED AFTER THE ROMAN KING OF GODS
NEPTUNE:
ONE YEAR ON NEPTUNE IS EQUAL TO NEARLY 165 EARTH YEARS
VENUS:
CLOSEST IN SIZE, MASS, AND DENSITY TO EARTH
MARS:
THE TALLEST MOUNTAIN ON MARS IS 16 MILES HIGH, ABOUT TWO AND A HALF TIMES HIGHER THAN MOUNT EVEREST

FACTS

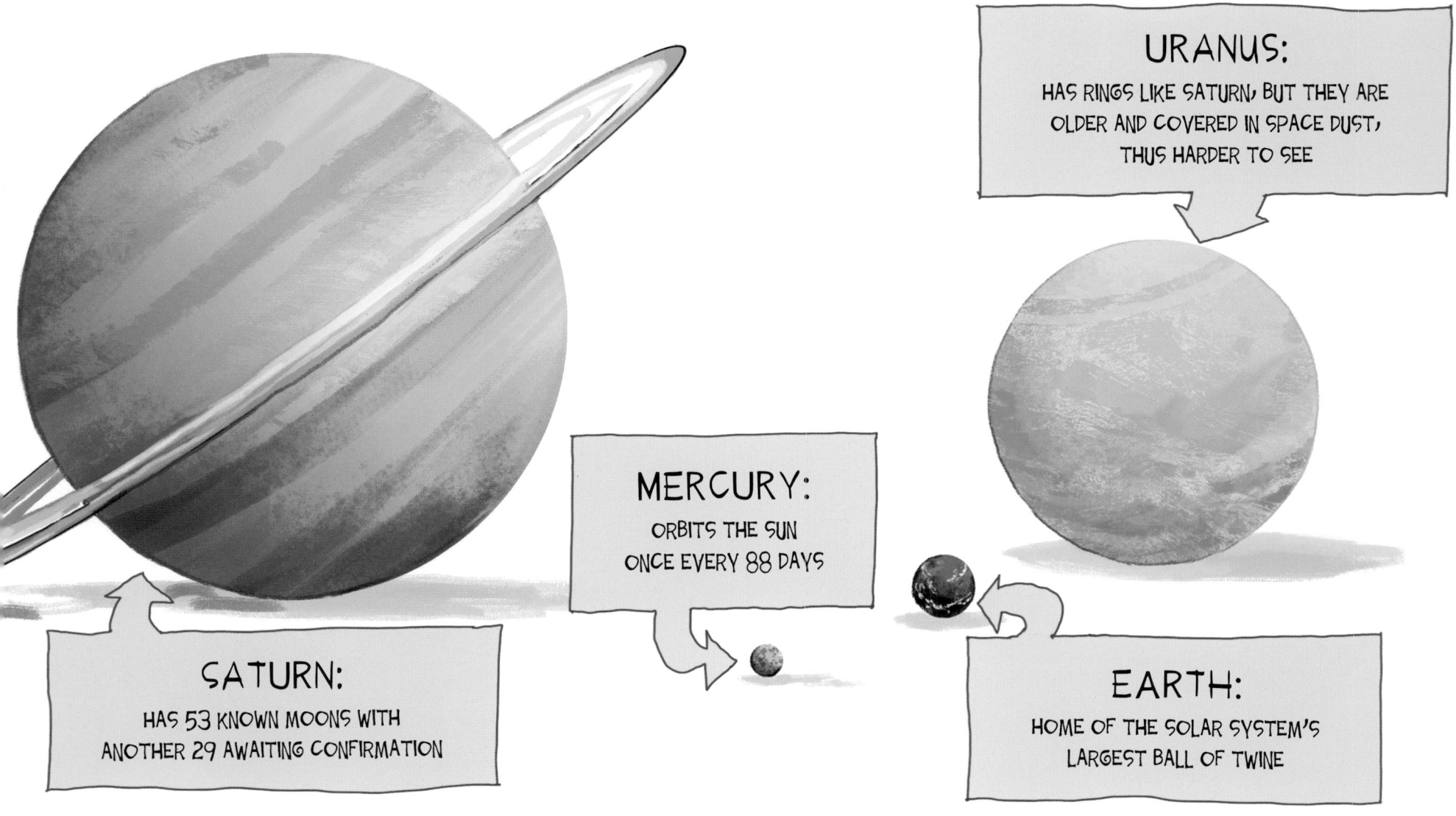
URANUS:
HAS RINGS LIKE SATURN, BUT THEY ARE OLDER AND COVERED IN SPACE DUST, THUS HARDER TO SEE
MERCURY:
ORBITS THE SUN ONCE EVERY 88 DAYS
SATURN:
HAS 53 KNOWN MOONS WITH ANOTHER 29 AWAITING CONFIRMATION
EARTH:
HOME OF THE SOLAR SYSTEM'S LARGEST BALL OF TWINE

MMM, JUST RIGHT.
I THINK I SPILLED PORRIDGE ON FINLAND.

THE
GOLDILOCKS
ZONE

AUTHOR'S NOTE:

Humans have always been fascinated by space. In the sixteenth century, Nicolaus Copernicus first suggested that Earth and the planets revolved around the Sun. It took several centuries and the work of astronomers, like Johannes Kepler and Galileo Galilei, before it was accepted as fact. The pace of space exploration has picked up a bit since then.

Since the middle of the twentieth century, humanity has launched the first satellite into orbit, sent men to the Moon, landed rovers on Mars, and there is still so much left to explore.

I'd like to thank the pioneering work of the scientists, engineers, and educators who made it possible for me to research a book about outer space from the comfort of my home here on Earth. Because, as you're about to find out, space is not known for its hospitality.

Special thanks to Dr. Jacqueline Faherty of the American Museum of Natural History for her expert review of the material.

For Alex. Space pants!

The Goldilocks Zone • Copyright © 2021 by Drew Sheneman • All rights reserved. Manufactured in Italy • No part of this book may be used or reproduced in any manner whatsoever without written permission except in the case of brief quotations embodied in critical articles and reviews • For information address HarperCollins Children's Books, a division of HarperCollins Publishers, 195 Broadway, New York, NY 10007. www.harpercollinschildrens.com • Library of Congress Control Number: 2020911620 • ISBN 978-0-06-297236-1.
Design by Drew Sheneman and Chelsea C. Donaldson • 21 22 23 24 PTLO 10 9 8 7 6 5 4 3 2 1 ❖ First Edition